MUSKRATS

Amy-Jane Beer

Grolier
an imprint of

www.scholastic.com/librarypublishing

Published 2008 by Grolier
An imprint of Scholastic Library Publishing
Old Sherman Turnpike, Danbury,
Connecticut 06816

For The Brown Reference Group plc
Project Editor: Jolyon Goddard
Copy-editors: Tom Jackson, Cécile Landau
Picture Researcher: Clare Newman
Designers: Jeni Child, Lynne Ross,
    Sarah Williams
Managing Editor: Bridget Giles

Volume ISBN-13: 978-0-7172-6273-1
Volume ISBN-10: 0-7172-6273-1

**Library of Congress
Cataloging-in-Publication Data**

Nature's children. Set 3.
    p. cm.
    Includes bibliographical references and
index.
    ISBN 13: 978-0-7172-8082-7
    ISBN 10: 0-7172-8082-9
    1. Animals--Encyclopedias, Juvenile. 1.
    Grolier Educational (Firm)
    QL49.N384 2008
    590.3--dc22
                            2007031568

Printed and bound in China

PICTURE CREDITS

Front Cover: **Superstock**: Age Fotostock.

Back Cover: **NHPA**: Yves Lanceau;
Photolibrary.com: Hamman/Heidring;
Superstock: Age Fotostock; **Shutterstock**:
John Czenke.

Alamy: Arco Images 33, John Cancalosi 38;
FLPA: B. and C. Calhoun/BCI 42, Hugo
Willock/Foto Natura 37; **Nature PL**: John
Cancalosi 30, Adrian Davies 34, Barry
Mansell 6, 14, Kim Taylor 17, Tom Vezo 21;
NHPA: Thomas Kitchin and Victoria Hurst
29, Yves Lanceau 41; **Photolibrary.com**:
E. R. Degginger 22; **Shutterstock**: Bull's
Eye Arts 10, Tony Campbell 2–3, 45, John
Czenke 13; **Still Pictures**: BIOS/Claude
Balcaen 4, 46, John Cancalosi 9, 18, 26–27,
G. Delpho/Wildlife 5.

Contents

Fact File: Muskrats 4

Super Rat 7

Local Name 8

Handy Paws 11

Fringed Feet 12

Rudder Tail 15

Deep Breath 16

Toothy Grin 19

A Perfect Home 20

Waterside Address 23

Expert Builders 24

Wet Front Door 25

Feature Photo 26–27

A Meal Adrift 28

Evening Menu 31

Winter Survival 32

Beaver or Muskrat? 35

Causing a Stink 36

Hello Boys!. 39

Babies Galore. 40

Early Days. 43

Moving On. 44

A Coat to Die For. 47

Home and Abroad. 48

Words to Know 49

Find Out More 51

Index. 52

FACT FILE: Muskrats

Class	Mammals (Mammalia)
Order	Rodents (Rodentia)
Family	Rats and mice (Muridae)
Genus	*Ondatra*
Species	Muskrat (*Ondatra zibethicus*)
World distribution	North America, with introduced populations in Europe and South America
Habitat	Slow-flowing rivers, pools, and marshes
Distinctive physical characteristics	A stout body; ratlike except for small ears hidden in fur and blunt snout; tail is long and scaly; fur is thick and rich brown
Habits	Mainly active at night; live alone or in small families; build lodges and floating feeding rafts out of water plants; spend much of winter asleep in a den in northern areas
Diet	Mainly water plants, but also small animals such as insect larvae, fish, and frogs

Introduction

What looks like a giant rat, but lives like a secretive beaver? The answer is a muskrat. This furry water lover lives by slow rivers, pools, and in marshes. It comes out mainly at night—so it can be difficult to see. In winter it spends all its time below the ice or inside specially constructed buildings. These structures have a hidden system of tunnels, chambers, and secret underwater entrances. A muskrat does not often come out in the open. That makes it difficult to watch muskrats, but luckily it is easy to see the signs that one is living in the area and producing babies.

Muskrats are common but difficult to spot in the wild.

A muskrat has a rounded face and body like a vole.

Super Rat

At up to two feet (60 cm) long from nose to tail tip, the muskrat is the largest member of the mouse family. As well as mice, this group includes, rats, lemmings, and voles.

The muskrat looks very much like a giant vole. Voles look like mice at first glance, but there are some noticeable differences between the two. Voles have small ears hidden in their fur, while mice have big round ears. Voles usually have a chubby face and a blunt snout, while mice have a longer pointed snout. Despite its ratty name, the muskrat definitely has a short blunt face and very small ears. It would actually be more accurately named the "muskvole"!

Local Name

Most people know muskrats by their common name. The animal takes its name from a stinky liquid called musk that the muskrat produces from a **gland** located just beneath its tail.

Biologists, however, know these stinky animals by another name—*Ondatra zibethicus*. Most animals have scientific names that come from Latin or Greek, but not *Ondatra*. This was the name given to the muskrat by the Native American Huron people, and European scientists decided to keep it.

The second part of the name, *zibethicus*, does come from Latin. It means "like a civet." Civets are spotted, catlike animals from Africa and Asia. What were those scientists thinking? Muskrats do not look anything like civets. But they do have one thing in common—musk. Both civets and muskrats emit a strong, musky odor.

Muskrats have oily fur that makes their coat waterproof.

As well as using
their paws for
feeding, muskrats
use them for
building nests.

Handy Paws

Imagine how much easier it would be for a rabbit to eat a carrot if its paws could pick up the food. Muskrats have front paws that can do just that. A muskrat's paws have fingers that allow them to hold small objects. However, their paws are not quite as good at gripping things as a monkey's or a human's hands are. That is because a muskrat's paws do not have thumbs that bend in the opposite direction to the fingers like human hands do. However, muskrats can still pick up things like seeds, twigs, and freshwater clams.

Fringed Feet

The muskrat's back feet are special, too. Some water animals, such as ducks and otters, have webbed feet to help them swim. A muskrat's toes do not have webs, because the skin of the webs would get damaged when the muskrat digs its **burrows**. Instead, the toes have a fringe of stiff hairs, which do the same job as webs. The fringe allows the muskrat to push much more water with each stroke, which enables it to swim surprisingly fast for an animal of its size. The fringe also helps spread out the muskrat's weight when it walks over soft ground. That prevents the muskrat from sinking into and getting stuck in the mud on the banks of rivers, streams, and lakes.

Muskrats swim by
paddling with all
four of their feet.

A muskrat's tail can grow to about 9½ inches (24 cm) long.

Rudder Tail

Muskrats have a long tail similar to the tail of common rats. However, a rat's tail is round from end to end, while a muskrat's tail looks as though it has been pushed in from the sides to form a long, flattened, oval shape, that is taller than it is wide. When swimming, the muskrat's flattened tail pushes against the water, which helps propel the animal swiftly along. A thin, rounded tail would push less water and, therefore, the animal would not be able to swim as quickly. The muskrat uses its tail like a rudder for steering while it swims. It can also swish its tail firmly from side to side for a burst of extra speed when needed. Top swimming speed for a muskrat is a little less than 3 miles (5 km) per hour. That is about as fast as a person walks.

Deep Breath

Humans can hold their breath underwater for an average of just under two minutes, although some champion swimmers and divers have been known to stay underwater without taking a breath for as long as four minutes. Muskrats can hold their breath and stay underwater for more than 15 minutes at a time! Usually they would only do that if something had frightened them and they needed to hide. A normal dive, when the muskrat looks for food or building materials for its home, lasts about three minutes—still a long time to go without breathing. While the muskrat is diving, its ears and nostrils close up so they do not become filled with water.

Apart from when it is in its burrow, a muskrat spends most of its time in water.

The muskrat's front teeth never stop growing. Gnawing wears them down and keeps them sharp.

Toothy Grin

Like other **rodents**—such as beavers, gophers, rats, and squirrels—muskrats have big front teeth. These large teeth are called **incisors** and while that can make the muskrat look a bit goofy, they are useful tools. The teeth are very, very sharp, which allow the muskrat to gnaw its way through the toughest plant stems—even solid wood.

Between the incisors and the muskrat's other teeth is a large gap. This gap allows the muskrat to close its lips behind its front teeth. That is very useful, because it means the muskrat can use its front teeth for digging without getting a mouthful of dirt. It can also carry building materials and food as it swims or dives, without swallowing water.

A Perfect Home

Muskrats like slow-flowing, fairly shallow
freshwater. If the water is moving too fast,
the plants muskrats like to eat get washed away
before they can grow. If the water is too deep,
not enough sunlight reaches the bottom for
young plants to grow. Muskrats can swim and
dive perfectly well in deep water. However,
they usually only do so to travel between good
feeding areas.

Water can be too shallow for muskrats as
well—very shallow pools are in danger of drying
up in summer or freezing solid in winter.

Muskrats can often be found around the
banks of pools or slow rivers where many cattails
grow on the bank. These plants give the muskrat
plenty to eat, a place to hide, and a good supply
of building materials.

Muskrats prefer feeding
places with thick reeds
for hiding in when
danger is near.

While some muskrats dig a burrow, others build a mud house, or lodge.

Waterside Address

Muskrats like to live very close to water. They often make a home by burrowing into the earthy banks of rivers and pools.

To make its burrow, a muskrat uses its front paws to dig. Its strong, long, front claws easily scoop out the damp clay or soil from the riverbank. If the muskrat comes across a tough root, it will gnaw it away with its sharp, front teeth. If it finds a stone blocking its way, it will remove it or dig around it. The entrance to the burrow is usually out of sight, hidden underwater. However, the muskrat burrows upward to hollow out a dry chamber, high above the water level, where it can sleep.

Expert Builders

Sometimes muskrats live in pools or marshes where there is no bank. Without a bank, the animal cannot build a burrow. But that does not stop them from setting up home. They simply build up an artificial bank out of twigs, water plants, and mud, then burrow into that. These types of homes are called lodges.

A muskrat lodge looks like a heap of rotten weeds and other plants at the water's edge. The muskrat spends many weeks collecting the plant material and mud to add to the pile, then when it is about three feet (1m) high, the muskrat dives underwater and begins burrowing into the mound from below, just as if it was a normal bank.

Wet Front Door

When muskrats dig burrows or build **lodges**, they always start the entrance underwater. The burrow slopes upward so that the sleeping chamber is always above the water and, therefore, stays dry. Having an entrance below the surface of the water ensures that **predators**, like foxes and mink, will most likely never see a muskrat hole. The muskrat hole is only ever visible if there is a long dry spell, and most of the river or pool the animal lives next to dries up. Usually the burrow entrance is far enough down for it to remain out of sight, even when the water level drops during a hot summer.

The underwater entrance also makes it unlikely that the muskrat will be trapped inside its burrow by ice, if the river or pool freezes over in winter. Water freezes from the top down. Even when the surface is frozen solid, the water several inches below is often still liquid, so the muskrat's door remains open.

A pair of muskrats sunbathe on top of their lodge.

A Meal Adrift

As well as lodges, muskrats also build rafts, which they use as floating **feeding stations**. Each raft is a small mat of woven twigs and reeds. The muskrat can climb onto the raft to rest and to eat the food it has collected during a dive. It is safer to feed on a raft floating in the middle of a pool than to sit on the bank. On land is where most of the muskrat's predators hunt.

The best time to watch muskrats is when they are sitting on their rafts feeding—they will stay in view as long as they feel safe. But if you come too close or startle them, they will plop into the water and disappear.

This muskrat has climbed aboard a passing log to eat its meal in peace.

A muskrat uses its sharp teeth to gnaw tough plant food.

Evening Menu

Muskrats usually rest during the day and come out at dusk to eat. Their favorite foods are plants that grow along the water's edge, such as cattails. Plants like that are usually easy to find, and they contain enough energy to keep the muskrat going. However, plant leaves and shoots do not contain very much **protein**, which animals need to grow, build muscles, and stay strong.

Muskrats get their protein by eating other animals. They rarely miss a chance to grab a passing insect **larva**, a small frog, or some juicy freshwater shellfish, such as clams and mussels. Female muskrats eat a lot of protein-rich foods to help them produce healthy babies.

Winter Survival

In winter, muskrats spend most of their time under the ice of frozen pools. They continue to feed on water plants. They often carry their food back to their dry burrow to eat. Muskrats also make holes in the ice so they can climb out of the water. Muskrats make these holes, called **push-ups**, when the ice is still very thin at the start of winter. They push pieces of plant stalk through the ice to make a large heap on the surface. The muskrat hollows out a space inside the heap, where it can feed in peace. By using the hole regularly and pushing more and more plants though it, the muskrat keeps the opening free of ice all winter.

Muskrats do not
hibernate during the
winter. They remain
active no matter
how harsh the
weather is.

Unlike muskrats, beavers are found naturally in Europe and Asia.

Beaver or Muskrat?

Muskrats are not the only water animals to build mud lodges and make heaps of plant material. Another fascinating rodent, the beaver, does the same types of things.

It is quite easy to get muskrats and beavers mixed up. Both of these animals are great swimmers, they both have brown, silky fur, and great big front teeth. In fact, the two animals are only distantly related, and there are many differences between the two. To start, beavers are two or three times bigger and ten times heavier than muskrats. Beavers also have a large paddle-shaped tail to help them swim. The muskrat has a long skinny tail.

Causing a Stink

The smell produced by muskrats is very important to them. To humans it is just an unpleasant odor, but to a muskrat it is like a whole conversation. In the same way you can learn a lot by listening to what someone says or by reading something they have written, a muskrat can sniff a musk-message left by another muskrat and take all sorts of meanings from it. To his male neighbors, a male muskrat might leave a message that says, "I still live here, and I'm very strong, so don't bother trying to invade my **territory**!" But to a female the same musk message says, "Hi there. We haven't met, but I think we should get together! I'm strong, I'm healthy, and I'd make a great dad for your babies!" The female might leave her own message in response.

Human's mix musk from muskrats with other chemicals to make perfumes.

Mates spend a long time smelling their partner as they get to know each other.

Hello Boys!

When a female is ready to **mate** and start a family, her male neighbors will be able to tell by the way she smells. Her scent will be spread all over the area, and it will often attract more than one male. These males will fight one another for the right to get close to the female. When there is only one male left—usually the strongest—the female will allow him to mate with her. The pair may share a burrow or lodge for a while. The babies are born about four weeks later. The mother usually kicks the father out of the burrow at this time to make more room in the nest. He will make a new burrow nearby so that he can be close when the female is ready to mate again in a couple of weeks.

Babies Galore

Muskrats can have an amazing number of babies. The number of babies in a **litter** varies, but it can be as many as 11. Because they grow up very quickly, the mother muskrat is able to have another litter a few weeks after the first litter arrives. Some females in the warmer regions have as many as 40 babies from six litters in a single year! Northern muskrats have fewer, smaller litters.

If muskrats breed so quickly and have so many babies, why is the world not overrun with these animals? The reason is a sad one—most baby muskrats die before they reach adulthood. Many of them get eaten by other animals. Some will be washed away and drowned by floods. Others will struggle to find a home because the best places already have muskrats living in them. The ones that survive long enough to set up a home and have families of their own are the lucky ones.

Newborn muskrats weigh three-quarters of an ounce (21 g).

Baby muskrats are fed milk by their mothers for less than four weeks. After that they must find their own food.

Early Days

Young muskrats are born with no fur and their eyes are shut tight. Their mother keeps them warm and dry. She also spends most of her time **nursing** them on her thick, fatty milk. With all this devoted care, the young muskrats grow up fast. Within just one week they have grown a full coat of fur and are scrambling about the nest. After two or three weeks the babies are ready to leave the nest. At this time they begin learning how to search for water plants to eat, just like their mother. After about six weeks they leave home for good. Their mother is ready for her young to leave—her next litter could be due any day.

Moving On

A huge number of young muskrats set out to find their own home each year. That means that good habitats are never empty for long. If a muskrat dies, it will be replaced in just a few days by another one, and if a new area of habitat appears, such as a bank made by a flood, a fishing pond, or a beaver lagoon, muskrats are among the first animals to move in.

When a young animal moves away from home in search of a new place to live, it is called **dispersing**. Dispersing is the most dangerous time in a muskrat's life. That's because it does not have a safe burrow or lodge to live in and might come across all sorts of dangerous situations before it finds somewhere to settle down.

A young muskrat sets off to find a place to make its home.

The oily outer hairs keep the undercoat dry. The dry undercoat keeps the animal warm even in icy water.

A Coat to Die For

Muskrat fur is beautiful. It is made up of two layers—a thick, soft undercoat of fine hairs and an outer coat of long hairs. The outer hairs are so oily that water runs off them the same way it does from a duck's feathers. People have always loved muskrat fur the same way they treasured the coats of beavers and mink. All these animals have been hunted and trapped for thousands of years so that humans can make luxurious, warm, waterproof clothing from their fur.

These days, with modern fabrics made in factories, there is no need for wild animals to die to make winter coats. Some people still like to wear fur, because they think it is more comfortable or makes them look good. Most of the fur worn today comes from farmed animals. Muskrats are smaller than other popular fur animals, and so they are rarely farmed for their fur today.

Home and Abroad

Muskrats live in most of North America. They range from Alaska across Canada, and throughout most of the United States. Not surprisingly they do not do so well in deserts because there are not enough pools and rivers for them to live in.

Muskrats turn up in other parts of the world, too. In the early 20th century, people took them to places like South America, Asia, and Europe to set up fur farms. That was a mistake, because the muskrats escaped and began to do a lot of damage in the wild. They feed on crops and garden plants and their burrowing weakened the banks of rivers, ponds, and irrigation canals, causing flooding. In Britain the problem was realized quickly and every muskrat was hunted down in the 1930s. Elsewhere it was already too late and countries like the Netherlands now have so many muskrats they can never all be caught.

Words to Know

Biologists   Scientists who study animals and plants.

Burrows   Animal homes dug into the earth.

Dispersing   The movement of young animals away from the place where they were born to find a new home.

Feeding stations   A floating raft where muskrats can feed safely.

Gland   A part of the body that produces a liquid, such as sweat, musk, or saliva.

Incisors   The teeth at the front of the mouth of muskrats and other mammals.

Larva   A young insect such as a grub.

Litter   A group of baby animals, all with the same mother.

Lodges	Heaps of water plants in which muskrats create a living space.
Mate	To come together to produce young; a breeding partner.
Nursing	Feeding young on milk.
Predators	Animals that hunt other animals for food.
Protein	An important part of the diet of most animals.
Push-ups	Winter feeding stations made above a hole in the ice of frozen pools.
Rodents	A very large group of gnawing mammals including mice, squirrels, and cavies.
Territory	The patch of land an animal treats as its private space and guards from others of the same species.

Find Out More

Books

Hall, M. *Muskrats*. Mankato, Minnesota: Capstone Press, 2004.

Kalman, B. *What Is a Rodent?* Science of Living Things. New York: Crabtree Publishing Company, 2000.

Web sites

Muskrat Facts
www.fcps.edu/islandcreekes/ecology/muskrat.htm
A lot of images of muskrats.

Talk About Wildlife
weaselhead.org/profile/index.php?s=547
Information about muskrats.

Index

A, B
Alaska 48
babies 5, 31, 39, 40, 41, 42, 43
beavers 5, 34, 35, 44, 47
breathing 16
burrows 12, 22, 23, 24, 25, 32, 39, 44

C, D
chambers 5, 23, 25
civets 8
claws 23
coat 9
danger 21
digging 12, 19, 22, 23, 25
dispersing 44
diving 16, 19, 20

E, F
ears 7, 16
entrances 5, 25
eyes 43
face 6, 7
feet 12, 13
fighting 39
fingers 11

food 16, 28, 29, 31, 32
fur 7, 9, 35, 43, 46, 47, 48

G, H, I
gland 8
gnawing 18, 19, 23, 30
habitat 5, 44, 48
hibernation 33
incisors 19

L, M
lemmings 7
length 7
litter 40, 43
lodge 22, 24, 28, 35, 39, 44
mating 39
milk 42, 43
musk 8, 36, 37

N, O, P
nest 10, 39, 43
nostrils 16
nursing 43
oil 9, 46, 47
paws 10, 11, 23
predators 25, 28
push-ups 32

R, S
rafts 28
rats 7, 15, 19
rodents 19
sleep 23
smell 36, 38
snout 7
sunbathing 26
swimming 12, 13, 15, 17, 19, 20

T, V, W
tail 8, 14, 15, 35
teeth 18, 19, 23, 30, 35
territory 36
trapping 47
tunnels 5
voles 6, 7
waterproofing 9